MLIMA'S TALE

MLIMA'S TALE

LYNN NOTTAGE

THEATRE COMMUNICATIONS GROUP   NEW YORK   2021

Mlima's Tale is published by Theatre Communications Group, Inc., 520 Eighth Avenue, 24th Floor, New York, NY 10018-4156

The publication of *Mlima's Tale* by Lynn Nottage, through TCG's Book Program, is made possible in part by the New York State Council on the Arts with the support of Governor Andrew Cuomo and the New York State Legislature.

Special thanks to The Repertory Theatre of St. Louis and its generous donors for their support of this publication.

TCG books are exclusively distributed to the book trade by Consortium Book Sales and Distribution.

Library of Congress Control Numbers:
2020017603 (print) / 2020017604 (ebook)
ISBN 978-1-55936-599-4 (paperback) / ISBN 978-1-55936-911-4 (ebook)
A catalog record for this book is available from the Library of Congress.

Book design and composition by Lisa Govan
Front cover design by Tammy Shell

First Edition, August 2021

For Melkamu Gerber

ACKNOWLEDGMENTS

Special thanks to Kathryn Bigelow, for her passion and guiding vision, and Patrick Milling Smith.

Based on the article "The Ivory Highway," by Damon Tabor, *Men's Journal*, February 13, 2014.

MLIMA'S TALE

PRODUCTION HISTORY

Mlima's Tale was originally developed and produced by The Public Theater (Oskar Eustis, Artistic Director; Patrick Willingham, Executive Director) in New York City, and had its world premiere on April 15, 2018. It was directed by Jo Bonney. The scenic design was by Riccardo Hernández, the costume design was by Jennifer Moeller, the lighting design was by Lap Chi Chu, the sound design was by Darron L. West, the hair and makeup design were by Cookie Jordan, the original music was by Justin Hicks; the movement director was Chris Walker, the fight director was Thomas Schall, and the production stage manager was Linda Marvel. The cast was:

MLIMA	Sahr Ngaujah
PLAYER 1	Kevin Mambo
PLAYER 2	Jojo Gonzalez
PLAYER 3	Ito Aghayere

Mlima's Tale had its regional premiere at Westport County Playhouse (Mark Lamos, Artistic Director; Michael Barker, Managing Director) in Westport, Connecticut, on October 1, 2019. It was directed by Mark Lamos. The scenic design was by Claire DeLiso, the costume design was by Fabian Fidel Aguilar, the lighting design was by Isabella Byrd, the projection design was by Yana Birÿkova; the composer was Michael Keck, the choreographer was Jeffrey Page, the fight director was Michael Rossmy, the props supervisor was Samantha Shoffner, the dialect coach was Julie Foh, and the production stage manager was Chris De Camillis. The cast was:

MLIMA	Jermaine Rowe
PLAYER 1	Jennean Farmer
PLAYER 2	Adit Dileep
PLAYER 3	Carl Hendrick Louis

NOTE

Four actors play all the roles.

If possible, a live musician should be present to augment the sounds of Mlima and the world at large.

The stage is a space that invites transformation, sparse and open. Perhaps projections and media can be used to give us a sense of place. The scene titles may be used as a design element. Scenes should fluidly collapse into each other.

There should be a breathless quality to the flow of the action, and as such no pure blackout until the end of the play.

A " // " indicates where overlapping dialogue should begin.

I

THUNDER IS NOT YET RAIN

A wilderness where a big tusker might seek refuge.
  The savannah. Full moon.
  Mlima, an elephant sensing danger, calls out to his fellow travelers.

MLIMA *(With intensity and urgency)*: When I was young I was
  taught by my grandmother to listen to the night. Really
  listen . . . for the rains in the distance . . . listen to the rustling of the brush . . . for the cries of friend or foe. She'd say
  you must listen with your entire body, feel how the earth
  shifts when there's the slightest disruption, because how
  you listen can mean the difference between life and death.
  It's the truth of the savannah, something we all learn at a
  very young age. Sacred words passed from generation to
  generation like stories of the verdant time before the vio-

lent crackle, before the drought and the madness . . . A time of plenty, when the plains and rivers were owned by all, a time recalled by my grandmother with such alacrity that one needn't be nostalgic. She'd say if you really listen, our entire history is on the wind.

(He listens and feels the night with his entire body, feet, ears, nose. Movement.
Slowly, the layers of sounds of the savannah fill the space.
The crickets, the orchestra of wild animals, cowbells, whistles, and the faraway voices of the Maasai.)

Even now, I hear the remnants of stories told by Long Ears, the elder, who knew where to find the sweetest acacia trees or the cool dark mud that was said to keep him ageless. When pushed he'd tell of how, once, he roamed so far across the land that it took him one year to find his way back home through the thorny thicket.

He returned with stories of rivers so wide they couldn't be crossed, trees so tall they did battle with the sky, and a sea of bobbing beasts and men. He'd walked across a world with no fences, no roads or resistance. We listened, though no one here believed such a far-fetched tale.

(Listens. Enjoying.)

I can hear the remnants of laughter, happiness that comes with the rains and reunions around the watering holes. Each hole a memory, a meeting, a sweet encounter, a fight and a friendship.

I hear my dear mother calling me handsome, but it was a *warning* that I'd come to understand as my tusks grew longer and more perfect than my brothers and sisters. I hear the first thunder that awakened me to fear. My first sneeze that accompanied the acrid stench of men. I hear the angry words exchanged before fighting Koko Mkimbiaji, we fought until we grew so tired that our only recourse was to become good friends. He made me laugh harder than any creature, even that gossipy egret who for a season clung to my back like a blemish.

(He listens with his body.)

Still now, I hear Koko Mkimbiaji wailing as his mother and sister died at the end of a poison spear, and anger became his guiding spirit. It took a year of wandering to calm him.

And I hear the song of beautiful Mumbi by the deep river, Mumbi elegant and quiet, brown liquid eyes. I chased her smell for a week, before she succumbed to my charm. Mumbi. Mumbi. Mumbi. I was not prepared for the first time we rubbed bodies, touched and committed. If you're listening, I could tell you of all the wounds I've endured for love.

I would share memories of the children we've sired and seen grow.

(His body begins to contort with pain. He grows restless.)

Mumbi, I'm sorry . . . so sorry that I haven't made myself known to you lately. I run more than I walk, and I can never catch my breath. They are watching me. Watching always. I hear them all around me. And I run, more than I walk.

Know I stay away from you and the children, because I'm protecting you. My distance is my weapon. I'm a shadow warrior all around you, listening to the sounds of the night. I hear everything. I hear you. I hear you.

(He charges across the stage. A warrior.)

(A battle cry) Aaaaaaaaaaaaaaa!

(He collapses and writhes in pain. He gets up and charges again.)

(A battle cry) Aaaaaaaaaaaaaaa!

II

EVEN THE NIGHT HAS EARS

Savannah. Moonlight.

    From a short distance, two Somali poachers, Rahman and Geedi, chewing khat, watch Mlima die. One man clutches a bow and arrow.

RAHMAN: Why won't he die already?

GEEDI: He's a fighter. He knows we've been hunting him.

RAHMAN: How?

GEEDI: He smells you.

RAHMAN: Me?

GEEDI: Yes. Your bush stink! Bulls smell their enemies from afar. Why do you think he's so difficult to track? He . . . he is an old one. A wanderer. Cleverer than most.

RAHMAN: You think he hears us?

GEEDI: Yes. He do.

(Mlima groans. Geedi looks him in the eyes.)

MLIMA *(Shouting/agony)*: If you're listening, remember, I count forty-eight rains from memory, five summers of dried grass. *(Grunts)*

RAHMAN: Why does he make too big noise?!

GEEDI: He's fighting. Battling death.

(Mlima cries out again in agony.)

MLIMA: If you can hear me, tell my children that I fought before death.

RAHMAN: Shoot him!

GEEDI: No. Don't want to waste bullets.

(Geedi spits.)

The gunshot, it'll call out the rangers. And I don't want that trouble tonight.

RAHMAN: Yare say give 'em beer, khat, they'll disappear quick quick.

GEEDI: For a man that never kill a thing bigger than the caterpillar yare have much opinions.

MLIMA *(Agony)*: Koko Mkimbiaji if you're listening. Don't come looking for me, my brother. Remember what I told you the last day of the rains. Let reason rule your anger, and don't come to mourn me! Run! Run!

RAHMAN: Too big noise.

MLIMA: RUN!

RAHMAN: Shoot him, Geedi.

GEEDI: No, it won't be long, give me the ax!

(Rahman spits and gives Geedi the ax.)

RAHMAN: Let's be quick quick about this. I don't like it here.

GEEDI: Be still. These last breaths don't belong to us.

RAHMAN: I never watch one die, not like this.

GEEDI: Poison better. You'll thank me.

(Geedi spits.)

RAHMAN: He's so big.

GEEDI: They call him Mlima, the mountain.

RAHMAN: All these nights of quiet.

GEEDI: Yes. He give us a good run.

RAHMAN: I fear we'll go home like beggars, and my wife, she'll go back to her family with an empty belly.

GEEDI: Don't worry, Rahman, you family'll be fed.

(Geedi squats next to the writhing Mlima.)

You hard to find, my friend. You think you is cleverer than me. You rob us of forty good nights spent in the wet bush. But, you make us rich rich.

MLIMA *(Shouting/agony)*: If you're listening, remember, I was once a proud warrior, unafraid to been seen.

GEEDI: Shhh. Don't fight. Don't. Don't fight.

MLIMA: I . . . AM . . . I—

GEEDI: Shh.

(Mlima groans. Geedi chops the elephant's face with the ax. Blood. Cries of agony. Silence.)

RAHMAN: You think it true, what Maasai say?

GEEDI: What that?

RAHMAN: If you not give elephant proper burial he'll haunt you forever.

GEEDI: They infidel. I no believe it.

RAHMAN: But, you . . . you certain?

GEEDI: Yes. My father took me on my first hunt when I be eleven. He guide white infidel from overseas. This man want to kill bull elephant. He carry a big big gun, too big, but still he afraid. Afraid of night sound. Afraid of the wind in the high grass. This is back when you kill elephant and no one trouble you.

(Geedi imitates a hyena.)

My father laugh at this man, but take his good money. He tell me that there be no sport in killing elephant, unless you kill with bow and arrow, spear, like warrior. It is creature to be respected, you must look it in the eye as it die. Give it the honor of knowing the hand that sent him to the other side. Right there. *(Points to the chest of the dying creature)* That's where my father stick 'em, between the leg and chest. And the poison it take elephant, give it long sleep. He say only infidel or white man kill elephant for sport. He teach me hunger be the only reason to kill.

RAHMAN: So, he no haunt us?

GEEDI: That's up to you, Rahman. I know where I stand, and I will sleep at night.

(Rahman stares at the bloody Mlima, disgusted.)

You okay?

RAHMAN: . . . Yes

GEEDI: Yes?

RAHMAN: I feel sorry, sometime.

GEEDI: You'll starve off of sentiments. Go fetch me a drink of water, this is going to take a long time.

RAHMAN: Okay.

(Rahman stares at the dead Mlima.)

GEEDI: Go! And don't forget the shovel.

(Rahman exits. Geedi begins to butcher Mlima, cutting out his majestic tusks. His trophies.

Mlima slowly transforms into the tusks, streaking his face and body with ivory paint or dust in a ritualized manner.

Over the course of the play Mlima continues to transform, becoming whiter. However traces of his brown skin should always be visible.

As Mlima journeys through the play, he leaves a white streak of paint or dust on every person he encounters. Residue. A stain. A mark of complicity. It should be visible to the audience, and punctuate the storytelling.)

III

NO MATTER HOW FULL THE RIVER, IT STILL WANTS TO GROW

Porch. Dawn.

    Githinji, an immaculately dressed Kenyan man, sits on an oversized wicker chair fanning himself with a Maasai fly swatter. He gives off an air of importance.

GITHINJI *(Furious)*: You gave me a list, and I responded. How could I've been so grossly misunderstood. I provided you with what you needed, yes? Guns, ammunition, supplies for twenty-five days, everything you needed, right? I'm looking at my calendar every single day, you know what it's saying to me, "Maybe this man has robbed me, because it's been forty days that I count and I've heard nothing until now."

(Lights rise on Geedi with the tusks, which from now on will be represented onstage by the actor playing Mlima.)

GEEDI: We—

GITHINJI *(Shouts)*: No, no, no . . . don't say anything, I'm speaking. What did I ask for? Huh? Eight tusks? And what do you bring me? Two. In your opinion is that acceptable? Yes, I am asking you? Is that acceptable? Now is when you may respond!

GEEDI: I swear to God, I bring you something better.

(He displays Mlima.)

GITHINJI: . . .

GEEDI: 2.4 meters. Ninety kilos each. They big big tusks in all Africa. The bull hide for reason. And he no easy capture. On he body, I count ten gunshot holes, I no first to try. But, Geedi the best tracker.

GITHINJI: You're very pleased with yourself.

GEEDI: Two tusks worth ten. And I expect to be paid just so.

GITHINJI: No.

GEEDI: No?

GITHINJI: You know why I say no?

(Githinji stands.)

GEEDI *(Perplexed)*: . . .

GITHINJI: You know why?

(Githinji rises, smacks Geedi.)

GEEDI: Boss?

GITHINJI: Do you know what you've done?

GEEDI: . . . Make you rich like white man?

GITHINJI: You bloody idiot. Who gave you the authority to kill Mlima? He's one of the last big tuskers in Kenya. Do you think it'll be easy for me to move these without notice? Every pair of eyes in this country will be looking for these tusks, every *(Shouting) warden*, every customs *agent*, every *dealer*, every *buyer, everyone*, goddamnit! I ask for eight tusks, that's four elephants, that's all I need, and your answer was, what?

GEEDI: . . .

GITHINJI: "No problem, boss." I communicated this to my buyers, who are very eager. I promised them that I would complete their order. I run a business. I have expectations, because my bosses have expectations. It's that simple. *(Shouting) But*, when you say to me, "No problem," that's what I expect. I don't care why you do what you do, I don't even care how many hungry children you have to feed, I don't care if your Allah demands that you do this for your jihad, all I care is that when we have an agreement, that it's honored.

GEEDI: Mr. Githinji, with all due respect, many people will pay good money for these.

GITHINJI: And they would be fools.

(A moment.)

GEEDI: Fifty thousand shillings for the pair.

GITHINJI: What?! Are you mad? You're lucky if I pay you anything, jackass! Do you know the trouble that you've made for me? And you still owe me six good tusks.

GEEDI: If you have problem, I go take elsewhere.

GITHINJI: I'm sorry you must repeat yourself, I don't think I heard you right.

(Githinji unburdens his pistol and rests it on his lap.)

GEEDI: Forty thousand shillings.

GITHINJI: You don't do business here, unless I invite you to do business here. Let's look at this situation. Okay? You've killed Mlima. They're going to be looking for his killer. You will be the most wanted man in Kenya. And when I tell them a Somali did it, ay! And the only thing standing between you and the authorities is me. To be clear, I'll do you the *favor* of taking the tusks off of your hands. That is what I'll do for you. But for now, we had an agreement. And as far as I am concerned you've not honored it.

GEEDI: But, Mr. Githinji—

GITHINJI: No, no but.

GEEDI: Can—

GITHINJI: I've stopped listening. I hear nothing. A mosquito. We're finished.

GEEDI: I spent forty days in the bush, got men to pay. You must offer me something. Or I'll go—

GITHINJI: What?!

(A moment. Githinji gently touches his pistol, then he reaches into his wallet.)

Okay. Twenty-four thousand. That is the best I can do.

GEEDI: But—

GITHINJI: You'll get the rest when you complete the job. Make sure that some of that money gets home to your mother. I don't want to hear that you and your Somali friends are rustling in my area again. Finish the job, and I may have some more work for you very soon. In the meantime be cautious. No celebrating.

(Geedi leaves defeated. Githinji smiles broadly, as if for the first time. Celebration. He stares at Mlima, who touches Githinji, leaving his white mark.)

IV

THE TEETH ARE SMILING, BUT IS THE HEART?

Sparse office. A single light bulb dangles from the ceiling. A fan churns out warm air.

    Wamwara, the regional warden, and Githinji sit, enjoying a laugh.

WAMWARA: I'm so sorry that we didn't make it to your birthday celebration this weekend. I've heard you roasted, what was it? Three goats.

GITHINJI: Four. You missed a good good party.

WAMWARA: Was Moses there?

GITHINJI: Yes, and so fat and pleased with his belly. Every time he sat down one more button popped off of his shirt. By the end of the evening he was parading his bare stomach like Buddha in paradise. Ah, you missed a party.

WAMWARA: I know, I know. This terrible business in the park, rains, early migration has brought the animals and the tourists, and I don't know which give me more trouble.

GITHINJI: How are things looking this season?

WAMWARA: . . . We'll see.

GITHINJI: Some whiskey?

WAMWARA: It's a little early, but . . . who am I to argue.

(Githinji pulls out a bottle of premium Jack Daniels and two cups from his desk.)

GITHINJI: This okay?

WAMWARA: Thank you. One . . . and half fingers.

GITHINJI: Two.

So . . . tell me why—

WAMWARA: Do I really have to tell you, Githinji?

(A moment. Githinji pours them each Jack Daniels.)

GITHINJI: My answer is no . . . No.

WAMWARA: No?

GITHINJI: No. You seem surprised.

WAMWARA: . . . It's just—

GITHINJI: Wamwara, is that what you think of me? I'm hurt by the implication.

WAMWARA: I'm sorry to bring up this ugly matter.

GITHINJI: You're upset, I don't blame you. But it's not how I do business. I wouldn't tamper with Mlima. That's why you're here, am I right? I know how important he is to the park. To Kenya for that matter.

WAMWARA: Yes. This is a real tragedy. Serious. I mean serious. He was one of our last big tuskers, you know.

GITHINJI: Awful—

WAMWARA: Unfortunately, there's gonna be a lot of scrutiny from very high up. They'll want us to find his killers. And someone must answer, and I'm directly in the firing line.

GITHINJI: Well, I'm not a fool, despite what your wife says.

(Githinji offers a smile to break the tension.)

WAMWARA: I'm serious. You must've heard something.

GITHINJI: Everyone knows that mighty Mlima was tagged and tracked with all of that special expensive equipment that your people bought. For too much good money if you ask me. Give the Maasai a cow and they'll do a better job tracking than your satellites.

WAMWARA *(A long exhale):* . . .

GITHIINJI: So, when did it happen?

WAMWARA: We lost his signal eleven days ago. I sent out some people last Wednesday and my men found him dead on Friday. Butchered beyond recognition. Every time this happens I feel the same wave of sadness, it always catches me off guard. But this time it really hurts.

(Wamwara is suddenly emotional. We feel Mlima's presence.)

I tell myself that he's just an animal, but I've been charged with protecting him, and I feel . . . .

(Wamwara weeps.)

I'm sorry.

GITHINJI: . . .

WAMWARA: Helpless.

(Githinji pours more whiskey for Wamwara. Wamwara pushes it away.)

We'll go public in two days. But we want to find those responsible before we face the media vultures. Look.

(Wamwara shows Githinji pictures of Mlima.)

GITHINJI: Good God.

WAMWARA: Please. Do you know who did this?

GITHINJI *(Lying)*: Your guess is as good as mine, perhaps an angry farmer.

WAMWARA: I don't think so—

GITHINJI: Lately, they've been lining up to complain, between the rains and the elephants stampeding, they've grown tired of losing their crops. People are angry, hungry—

WAMWARA: No, no, no, these were professionals. Might it be Somalis?!

GITHINJI: I don't know. Every day I have villagers coming to me, because the thieving raiders are stealing their cattle and disappearing over the border. Every day! I'm not paid to fight a war. I used to be able to police with a big stick, now every farmer has a gun and a grudge to be settled. And I don't do business with gangsters.

WAMWARA: A man of principles, huh?

GITHINJI: This nonsense is bad for all of us. I'm the chief of police. What example would I be setting if I allowed this kind of business to happen in my backyard? Poachers invite problems.

(Githinji pours himself another whiskey.)

WAMWARA: Your window looks over the road to Mombasa, nothing passes without your watchful eye.

(Githinji sips his drink, considers.)

GITHINJI: . . .

WAMWARA: You must—

GITHINJI: Let me investigate, interrogate a few of the known poachers and traffickers.

WAMWARA: That would be very helpful. Mlima was a much beloved creature. Perhaps too obstinate and set in his ways for his own good.

GITHINJI: True enough. You okay? How are you holding up?

WAMWARA: My rangers mourn. And I worry. They're already demoralized. This is a really big loss for them.

GITHINJI: I'm sorry.

WAMWARA: My boss asks why we can't do better? It's my duty to protect, but I have a mere handful of men covering an area that is twenty-two thousand square kilometers. And I'm running on vapors.

GITHINJI: What is done is done. I know you did your best. Let us look to the future.

WAMWARA (*Emotionally*): Yes. This may seem foolish, but I don't want Mlima's tusks to leave Kenya. It would be a tremendous dishonor. They should be buried here in our park with his body. We owe him that respect.

GITHINJI: I promise you. I'll do whatever I can to find the culprits.

WAMWARA: Unfortunately, this is going to invite the eyes of the international community. And you know how these white people love their animals.

GITHINJI: Too much in my opinion. They buy their dogs food from the supermarket. It costs more than most Kenyans make in a week.

WAMWARA: Yes—

GITHINJI: Ask me, the only reason to bring an animal into your home is to make a stew.

(Githinji laughs, Wamwara manages a faint smile.)

Don't let this thing weigh you down. I'll get to the bottom of it for you.

WAMWARA: I just need something.

GITHINJI: I will take care of it. Enough of this business. How's the family?

WAMWARA: Good, Uncle. Things are always a little tight around this time of year. School fees, you know the drill.

GITHINJI: They grow too fast.

WAMWARA: Yes.

(Githinji casually reaches into his desk, and passes Wamwara an envelope across the table.)

That may help.

WAMWARA: Is that what you think I'm here for?

GITHINJI: . . .

WAMWARA: No. Not this time.

GITHINJI: C'mon. Don't thank me. It's a gift from your favorite uncle. That's all.

(Wamwara studies the envelope, fighting temptation.)

Put new tires on your truck.

WAMWARA: . . .

GITHINJI: It'll make things easier for . . . everyone.

WAMWARA: . . .

(Wamwara continues to stare at the envelope, but doesn't pick it up. Simmering.)

I don't know what you know *(Sudden rage, shouting)* but, it *has to stop!*

GITHINJI *(Suddenly stern)*: I don't like what you're implying.

WAMWARA: Nor do I like what you're implying.

GITHINJI: WE'RE NOT SCHOOLBOYS HERE!

(A moment. Wamwara asserts his power.)

WAMWARA: I don't want to quarrel. There's a lot of pressure on me. This is my territory, my park. What was done was *disrespectful.* Mlima was under the protection of *my* people. I've been patient, I think. There are plenty of other ways to make yourself fat and comfortable.

GITHINJI: You overstate.

WAMWARA: I know my jurisdiction doesn't extend beyond the park, but yours does. And, I'm asking you to make this right. As my family, my uncle, I'm asking you to give me some help. Anything. One name. My job is on the line.

GITHINJI *(A quandary)*: . . .

WAMWARA: A warning! They're going be watching the roads, the ports. Everywhere. So if you know something, perhaps it's best to share it now.

GITHINJI: I understand your anger, but—

WAMWARA: You understand nothing. I promise you, I'm not going to allow Mlima to leave here without a fight. I won't let them make him into a trinket.

(Wamwara storms out. Githinji ponders. Mlima looms in the half light.)

V

A SINGLE STICK MAY SMOKE, BUT IT WILL NOT BURN

Nairobi. A clean sleek air-conditioned office. Phosphorescent lights and wildlife posters.

Andrew Graves, a white Kenyan, director of wildlife, sits on his desk. He is a man comfortable with his authority. He's in a meeting with Wamwara.

ANDREW: Do you think it should be more personal? Begin with an anecdote or something about poor Mlima. Jesus! This is impossible. Okay . . . *(Reading from his speech)* "We're under siege. A war is being waged against the elephants in our country. It's a matter of national security." Bla, bla, bla. "We're standing on the edge." Edge?

WAMWARA: Precipice?

ANDREW *(Correcting)*: Precipice, yes. "We . . . we can't stand by as our most precious resources are systematically being destroyed." *(Reading quickly now)* "Poachers plunder with impunity. Ivory trafficking has decimated our elephant population. Forty-five years ago there were 1.3 million elephants roaming the plains and forests of Africa, today there are less than four hundred thousand. The maths are simple. There are more elephants being killed than are being born, which means that in less than twenty years they may well be extinct." Too much you think?

WAMWARA: No, Andrew, it's very strong. Direct.

ANDREW: I worry. I've made this speech one too many times, Wamwara. But these damn statistics keep outrunning me.

WAMWARA: I always write them on a card in case I get flustered. Journalists, they're a tricky bunch.

ANDREW: True enough. Particularly that pretty reporter who's always so bloody aggressive.

WAMWARA: Patience Wainana.

ANDREW: That's the one . . .

WAMWARA: Andrew, I want you to know we worked very hard to protect Mlima.

ANDREW: Then goddamnit who fell sleep at the wheel?

WAMWARA *(Contrite)*: I have a good team . . . All of our systems were in place, it was working. But, Mlima was too smart and independent, which is why he was so impossible to protect.

ANDREW: A clever elephant and an apology aren't going to be sufficient this time. There will be fallout—

WAMWARA: I understand.

ANDREW: And your Uncle Githinji?

WAMWARA: He gave me three poachers, little fish, otherwise he says he knows nothing more.

ANDREW: Rubbish! That lying piece of shit. I'm sorry, I know you're related, but he's the most corrupt contemptible bastard.

WAMWARA: That may be true, but he firmly denies being involved.

ANDREW: Then that's a bigger problem for us. Go back, talk to him. No one collects pebbles on the road to Mombasa without paying him a toll. Push! And you have my permission to fucking shoot him if you have to.

WAMWARA: I have his word. He blames the Somalis.

ANDREW: And do you?

WAMWARA: . . .

ANDREW: Well?

WAMWARA: I don't know. This is all one big headache. In the west of the park we have the Maasai to contend with, they're overgrazing their cattle. To the east the border, and all of the chaos that that brings. I don't know how we're supposed to keep the animals secure under these circumstances.

ANDREW: Fucking hell.

WAMWARA: The poachers are better organized. And the truth is we don't have enough rangers to put out every bushfire that God can conjure, I feel—

ANDREW: Stop! I'm sick of excuses. My wife thinks we should offer a generous bounty. Smoke the bastards out.

WAMWARA: With all due respect, my rangers won't stand for that. Remember, several of my best men have given up their lives protecting animals this year, and they did it for very little reward. You'll have a mutiny.

ANDREW: Okay! Calm down. Of course, I haven't forgotten. But, in two hours I have to get up in front of those cameras and explain how some bloody idiots snuck into my park and killed one of our national treasures. One of our last great tuskers. How pathetic will I look if I go out there and tell them this is all just one big headache.

WAMWARA: We're not sitting still. We captured three poachers, they're in custody, the fourth was killed in a fire fight. Poor Nigel was seriously wounded.

ANDREW: I heard. Terrible. How's his family holding up?

WAMWARA: We took a collection. He'll be in hospital until the end of the month.

ANDREW: Let me know how much I should give. I'd like to.

WAMWARA: Of course.

ANDREW: But, I need something, Wamwara! NOW! Did you at least recover Mlima's tusks?

WAMWARA: . . . No. But we did confiscate four small tusks from two young bulls. We haven't located the carcasses yet.

ANDREW: Fucking hell! Explain to me how your men can be so willfully incompetent?

WAMWARA: My men are in the process of interrogating // the poachers. They are . . .

ANDREW: Yes. Yes. Yes. Fine. But all I want to know is, could these be our culprits?

WAMWARA: . . . No. Amateurs. But, it is something.

ANDREW *(Impatient)*: I don't think you understood what I was asking. I need more than conjecture. So, I'm going to ask you again, are these the poachers that killed Mlima?!

(A moment. Wamwara contemplates the question. Mlima appears, an imposing presence.)

WAMWARA: . . . Yes.

ANDREW: Good. Well done. I'm tired of the media and those conservation fascists accusing us of being impotent. They're all very vocal from behind their stacks of paper. Let them face down the bullets.

WAMWARA: But—

ANDREW: Now, at least, we have something to offer. I'll shame the government officials for not providing us with sufficient funds, move the focus away from us.

WAMWARA: Yes.

ANDREW: Point the finger at corruption, and their failures to prosecute traffickers.

WAMWARA: It'll make them angry.

ANDREW: Good, let them pick up the slack. Make them a little scared.

But, between you and me, I want whoever's responsible for killing Mlima found. Someone gave the order and I hate that they're still out there. Find them.

(Wamwara exits. Andrew finds himself facing the flashbulbs. The sound of a crowd gathering.)

"It is with great sadness and regret that I report the death of our beloved Mlima."

VI

A WORD IS LIKE THE DELTA, IT STRETCHES
IN EVERY DIRECTION

Press conference. The reporters, Guoxi and Patience, ask questions.
Camera lights.

GUOXI *(Aggressively)*: I'm curious, how is it possible that Kenya's
  most famous elephant could be slaughtered beneath the
  noses of an army of KWS rangers?
ANDREW: As I already said, we've arrested two poachers in
  connection with the killing of Mlima. My men should be
  commended for how swiftly they apprehended the culprits.
  I'd like to recognize the quick work of Warden Wamwara
  Machau. It's now up to our government to ensure that the
  poachers are brought to justice, and that the criminal syndi-
  cates that fund them are targeted and shut down. Our duty
  is to protect wildlife. We're conservationists. Our reach

doesn't extend into the government buildings, markets and homes of people responsible for driving the demand.

PATIENCE: Are you certain that these are the men responsible?

ANDREW: . . . That is a complicated question. Did they kill Mlima, yes, are they solely responsible . . . no.

PATIENCE: You keep evading questions! Why has it been so easy for poachers to track and kill elephants in your park?

ANDREW (*Flustered—snaps*): It's not easy. They're experts. They are determined, and in some cases desperate. Some of them have equipment that surpasses our own. They strike at night, when elephants like to travel, and we don't have the resources to track all of the animals in every park. Poachers are clever, believe it or not, they're even using social media, tourist photos to locate elephants.

One last question!

(*Mlima climbs onto Andrew's shoulders. Andrew feels the weight.*)

GUOXI: Are you overstating perhaps to hide the fact that your agency has not done enough? It is easy to place blame elsewhere?

ANDREW: Again, who are you?

GUOXI: Fu Guoxi, information and public affairs, Chinese Embassy.

(*As Andrew speaks we begin to hear cocktail chatter, traditional Chinese music.*)

ANDREW: To stop ivory trafficking will require all of the security agencies to collaborate, and that has proven very difficult. We—and I speak of all of us—must eliminate the corruption that allows this to continue in our country. It is a matter of national pride! Africans don't buy ivory.

VII

NO ONE TESTS THE DEPTH OF THE RIVER
WITH BOTH FEET

Cocktail party. Chinese Embassy.
    A local musician provides ambiance. Applause. Hassan Abdulla,
a smartly dressed Tanzanian businessman from Zanzibar, holds court.

GUOXI: To be one hundred percent honest, I am relatively new.
    I was reluctant to leave Beijing and take this position.
    I didn't know very much about Africa. But now it will be
    very difficult to leave. And you?

HASSAN ABDULLA *(Speaks self-consciously; this is not his indigenous*
    tongue): I was a promising football player, it's why I first
    traveled to Asia. An injury curtailed my ambition. I was,
    how do I say it? Forced to make an adjustment. One door
    closed, another door opened. You see the world, you get

ideas, but sometimes I still wish I had the innocence of my relatives who live in a village so remote that it has no road.

GUOXI: Your Chinese is very good. I am always pleased when I meet a foreigner who speaks my language.

HASSAN ABDULLA: It comes with its advantages. These days in Nairobi there are many more people with whom I can practice.

GUOXI: Are you part of the Builders Consortium?

HASSAN ABDULLA: Oh no.

GUOXI: Hmm, so, how did you come to this event at our embassy?

HASSAN ABDULLA: I'm a friend of Mr. Xu.

GUOXI: Oh. Yes. He's a dear friend of mine as well.

HASSAN ABDULLA: Then we have something in common, and that is fortuitous. Lucky us. I'm Hassan Abdulla, I'm . . . a businessman. My company is HB Global Group. Based here, and in my home, Zanzibar. My card.

GUOXI: Thank you. Fu Guoxi. Mine.

(They go through the ritual of exchanging cards.)

Excuse me.

(Guoxi goes to exit.)

HASSAN ABDULLA: Mr. Fu, how do you find Nairobi?

GUOXI: I like it very much. More cosmopolitan than I expected, very green. I've learned there are many things people get wrong about Africa. The climate here is quite pleasant and the people are very welcoming.

HASSAN ABDULLA: We're at a high elevation. Few mosquitoes. Cool air. Very beautiful.

GUOXI: Yes. I enjoy it.

HASSAN ABDULLA: You must find that there are things that you can acquire here that are difficult to come by in China.

GUOXI: True enough. I'm still exploring.

HASSAN ABDULLA: Are you a collector of—

(A caterer interrupts with a tray of samosas.)

. . . African art?

GUOXI: A beginner.

HASSAN ABDULLA: Like Mr. Xu.

GUOXI: Well. My interests are similar. Mr. Xu is an expert in African artifacts. Me, I'm simply looking for very special souvenirs to send home to the family.

HASSAN ABDULLA: I see. Let's move near the window, fresh air is welcome. Have you been on safari yet?

GUOXI: Yes. Lake Nakuru. Saw the flamingos.

HASSAN ABDULLA: Very beautiful.

GUOXI: And the Maasai Mara with my children.

HASSAN ABDULLA: Did you see the big five? Lion, leopard, cape buffalo, rhinoceros, and . . . um, elephant?

(They move.)

GUOXI: Ah, yes. Beautiful. In fact the other day I was at a press conference, and I heard the director of wildlife speak of a big tusker that was killed in Tsavo.

HASSAN ABDULLA: Mlima. Tragedy for Kenya—

GUOXI: And I hear they caught the culprits.

HASSAN ABDULLA: Praise be.

GUOXI: They say the tusks were amongst the largest in the world.

HASSAN ABDULLA: They were not recovered as far as I know.

GUOXI: Hm. I imagine they would be priceless on the market, no?

HASSAN ABDULLA: Not priceless, but very expensive—

GUOXI: Is that so?

HASSAN ABDULLA: You know, it's rare to find an elephant as old or as large as Mlima. His tusks were extraordinary.

(Mlima emerges from the shadows. He slowly circles Hassan Abdulla and Guoxi. He does a seductive dance as Guoxi speaks.)

GUOXI: I've seen them only in photos. A collector's dream. During the revolution many fine things were lost in China, but my grandfather managed to hold on to a beautiful ivory carving of Quan Yin, the goddess of compassion. The Buddhist statue was perfection. I believe, carved by one of the great masters in the seventeenth century. Quan Yin was hidden away for many years. There was a period when possessing such an exquisite sacred object branded you a criminal. But, when I was young, on very special occasions my grandfather would remove the statue from the bottom of an old trunk, carefully unwrap it from its shroud of cloth, place it on the table, and everyone in the family would gather. Gaze. Admire it. It was so . . . intricate, lovely. It felt like a rare blessing that had been bestowed on our family.

HASSAN ABDULLA: I should like to see it.

GUOXI: Not possible. It was destroyed during a fire. I must confess with some embarrassment that I have always wanted to find something to replace Quan Yin.

HASSAN ABDULLA: I understand the allure. As a matter of fact, I had ancestors that led caravans deep into the interior. They'd bring cloth and beads to trade with local chiefs. Sometimes, they'd even travel with two thousand porters. Do you know how much ivory two thousand people can carry? *(Laughs)* And they shame us today for the few sacrificed, forgetting that it's part of an ancient tradition, and a long history of trade between Asia and Africa.

GUOXI: Mr. Abdulla. I must stop you there. The direction of this conversation is making me very uncomfortable.

(Mlima retreats into the darkness.)

HASSAN ABDULLA: My apologies. I hope you haven't misinterpreted anything that I have said.

GUOXI: As long as we are clear. I am here in an official capacity for the embassy.

HASSAN ABDULLA: Then I do insist that you come visit my business on your day off. I specialize in all manner of collectibles. And I sense you have a discerning eye.

VIII

DON'T THINK THERE ARE NO CROCODILES
BECAUSE THE WATER IS CALM

*Simple beachside restaurant. Aziz Muhammed paces and shouts into
his cell phone.*

    Hassan Abdulla hovers in the background.

AZIZ MUHAMMED *(Shouting into his cell phone)*: What's his prob-
    lem? What's his problem? Put him on! No, I said put him.
    Stop. Stop. Put him on now!

(Aziz Muhammed signals for Hassan Abdulla to sit.)

One minute. *(Into the cell phone)* I don't care what they
want! No. Tell them it isn't possible. Are you crying? Tears
don't work with me. I'm drawing the line. They will get
no more money from me! Put him on! Listen, I will not

be threatened! It's extortion and I won't be pushed any further. *(To Hassan Abdulla, covering the cell phone)* Excuse me, my brother is getting married. The bride's family are like gangsters. *(Into the cell phone)* All this yelling is giving me a headache. I'm hanging up. *(He hangs up)* I'm so sorry, where were we?

HASSAN ABDULLA: No worries. I was—

AZIZ MUHAMMED: My younger brother is getting married next month. My father is deceased so I agreed to help with the arrangements. I made the mistake of having the bride's family over for dinner, and they saw my home and now they've decided that I'm a rich man. They keep increasing the demands. I think this foolishness is outdated. But, the girl's mother wants a new refrigerator, the most expensive one from the catalog, and her father wants some chair with a built-in back massage. What is this craziness?

She's a modern woman in every respect, until it comes to this nonsense, then suddenly she is talking about tradition. Ay. I swear to God, these people. I might shoot someone before all this is done?

(Hassan Abdulla laughs.)

You think I am kidding? Watch. The demands will never end. Stop laughing, this is killing me. Ay. How long have you been married?

HASSAN ABDULLA: Fifteen years.

AZIZ MUHAMMED: Ay! Fifteen years, which is fourteen years too many in my opinion.

(A moment.)

So—

HASSAN ABDULLA: What do you think?

AZIZ MUHAMMED: I don't like it. Not now. Timing feels bad.

HASSAN ABDULLA: Why?

AZIZ MUHAMMED: Heat is everywhere. It's dangerous in Mombasa. Mlima is in the news every day. They are watching us.

HASSAN ABDULLA: I have a promising buyer. Someone well placed and a powerful ally, here and abroad.

AZIZ MUHAMMED: Why change plans now? I have our shipment at the warehouse ready to leave in six days. One ton. Everything has been arranged. And honestly, my timber boxes are not large enough to accommodate tusks that size. Remember, the only reason they arrested David Lao last year is because he second-guessed himself. Changing plans mid-stream is never a good idea, my friend.

HASSAN ABDULLA: Then we move ahead with the shipment, but . . . we could transport these tusks on a separate dhow. Meet the ship after it leaves dock. They are very precious—

AZIZ MUHAMMED: But very hot.

HASSAN ABDULLA: There is real money here!

AZIZ MUHAMMED: Settle down. Stop licking your lips. I appreciate it, but I can only manage one shipment at a time. My answer— No!

HASSAN ABDULLA: This Fu Guoxi is willing to pay an extra nine million five hundred thousand shillings for the pair.

AZIZ MUHAMMED: But is it worth the risk?

HASSAN ABDULLA: In my opinion. Yes.

AZIZ MUHAMMED (*Excited*): You trust this man Fu?

HASSAN ABDULLA: Yes.

AZIZ MUHAMMED: Who else knows that you have the tusks?

(*Mlima emerges from the shadows. He stares at Aziz Muhammed.*)

HASSAN ABDULLA: Githinji, my local handler, of course, and his transporters. But, they are scared. He practically dropped them on my doorstep.

AZIZ MUHAMMED (*Thinking*): I understand. But, the tusks are attracting too many flies. It's making me very nervous. I'm done.

(Aziz Muhammed looks back at Mlima almost as if he can see him.)

HASSAN ABDULLA: But, it is good for us.

AZIZ MUHAMMED: Maybe, we wait, let the dust settle, send the big shipment as planned, then float Mlima's tusks on the web. An auction.

HASSAN ABDULLA: No, Aziz. Listen! I want to be rid of them quickly. The longer I hold them the more my fingers hurt. And my buyer is eager to forge a relationship.

AZIZ MUHAMMED: I worry that someone may want to make their name on this confiscation. And I really don't want to be famous.

HASSAN ABDULLA: Our friend in the ministry has helped us before.

AZIZ MUHAMMED: Hmm. No. As is, they're way too large. Cut the tusks down, be rid of them.

(Mlima sits at the table with Hassan Abdulla.)

HASSAN ABDULLA: Absolutely not, we'd destroy their value. They are special. Perfectly symmetrical. This man will pay nine million five hundred thousand shillings for the pair. Nine million five hundred thousand. More than our other partners.

AZIZ MUHAMMED: 9.5? Huh?

HASSAN ABDULLA: Listen.

AZIZ MUHAMMED: Nine . . . five?

HASSAN ABDULLA: You can buy a warehouse of refrigerators.

AZIZ MUHAMMED: Okay. Okay. I get it. *(Smiling)* We have to proceed very cautiously. I don't trust the people at the docks.

(Aziz Muhammed's cell phone rings.)

Ah. What now? *(He answers)* I am in the middle of business! I'm not going to talk to her mother. No. NO!

(He hangs up.)

I'm sorry. My goodness. Are you hungry? Do you want to order something?

HASSAN ABDULLA: I'm fine.

AZIZ MUHAMMED: You sure? My treat. The food is okay here. Eat something.

HASSAN ABDULLA: I'm good. I'll eat at home. My wife thinks I'm out cheating if I don't take meals every night with her. It's too much trouble.

AZIZ MUHAMMED: Too much power for a woman.

(Aziz Muhammed laughs.)

Have you made payment arrangements?

HASSAN ABDULLA: Half of the money will be wired up front, the other half will be wired upon delivery to his people in Vietnam. Let's do this. I want to get the tusks out of Kenya as soon as possible.

AZIZ MUHAMMED: Okay. Between us.

IX

THE BEST WAY TO EAT AN ELEPHANT IN YOUR PATH IS TO CUT HIM INTO LITTLE PIECES

Mombasa port. A ship.
A haughty American, Captain Ramaaker, oversees the loading of cargo crates.

CAPTAIN RAMAAKER: No. No. NO! I'm running clean now. After what happened last week, I'm not taking any more chances. The police are all over the docks. Never seen it like this.

AZIZ MUHAMMED: Ramaaker, don't make this a big deal. I'll provide you with the appropriate permits and paperwork on this side. Don Loc Enterprises will have the necessary papers in Vietnam. It will run absolutely smoothly. I promise. So don't get bent out of shape. As far as you know it's just timber, same as always, but I need someone I can rely on.

CAPTAIN RAMAAKER: They're cracking down. We stop in Muscat, Port Klang, before Hai Phong. I could do real time for this.

AZIZ MUHAMMED: Don't worry, you have an American flag. They will look past you. Relax. Trust me. I have a dhow that will meet you offshore, just beyond the reach of the Kenyan authorities. It's just timber, that's all you need to know.

CAPTAIN RAMAAKER: My manifests are complete. If I add something now it will raise eyebrows.

AZIZ MUHAMMED: Don't worry about the paperwork.

CAPTAIN RAMAAKER (*Whistle*): No, stop, stop! Those need to be loaded last. Aziz, why do you always do this? You're going to give me a heart attack.

AZIZ MUHAMMED: Don't say that. You make it sound like I wish you dead.

(*Aziz Muhammed kisses Captain Ramaaker and hands him an envelope.*
Captain Ramaaker counts the money and hands it back.)

CAPTAIN RAMAAKER: . . . NO.

(*He begins to walk away. Aziz Muhammed firmly grabs him.*)

Please, don't touch me. We're not friends.

AZIZ MUHAMMED: I have been very helpful to you in the past.

CAPTAIN RAMAAKER: Don't keep bringing that up. My debt is paid. I don't want to be involved with this business.

AZIZ MUHAMMED: I need this favor. I can be insistent, but I'm confident you will see reason.

CAPTAIN RAMAAKER: It's too last minute, and that always scares me. What is the rush?

AZIZ MUHAMMED: It needs to be moved quickly.

CAPTAIN RAMAAKER: Why?

AZIZ MUHAMMED: Do you really need to know why?

CAPTAIN RAMAAKER: . . .

AZIZ MUHAMMED: I need discretion and I need my cargo moved this week, and with as few eyes as possible.

CAPTAIN RAMAAKER: Not this time! I'm sorry.

(Captain Ramaaker walks away.)

AZIZ MUHAMMED: Son of a whore!

(Chief Mate, Jim Baxter, sheepishly approaches Aziz Muhammed.)

CHIEF MATE: Mr. Muhammed?

AZIZ MUHAMMED: Do I know you?

CHIEF MATE: Jim Baxter, chief mate. We've meet several times. I know your brother, Abubar.

AZIZ MUHAMMED: Of course, Jimmy.

CHIEF MATE: I might be able to help you. Six percent is what I'm asking.

AZIZ MUHAMMED: Three.

CHIEF MATE: Four.

AZIZ MUHAMMED: Three and a half.

(Mlima looms over Chief Mate.)

CHIEF MATE: Tomorrow evening. When the captain turns in. I can load the container from the dhow. The captain does not need to know, he's not meticulous.

AZIZ MUHAMMED: Three and a half.

CHIEF MATE: I want to be paid up front.

AZIZ MUHAMMED: No. That's not how it works. Half and half. What spooked him?

CHIEF MATE: Some officials came on board. They put the fear of God in him.

AZIZ MUHAMMED: All they want is a small bribe.

CHIEF MATE: Apparently not. They are looking for Mlima's tusks. They feel insulted.

(Aziz Muhammed gives Chief Mate the envelope.)

AZIZ MUHAMMED: What time?
CHIEF MATE: Gimme your cell number, I'll send you the coordinates.

(Chief Mate leaves, Mlima follows him.)

X

DO NOT LOOK WHERE YOU FELL, BUT WHERE YOU SLIPPED

Cargo container moves to the rhythm of the restless ocean. The faint fragmentary voices, elephant memories fill the space.

FAINT LAYERED VOICES:
    Kade, son of Gatimu,
    Kabonessa, daughter of Kiserian,
    Lakenua, mother of Namelok,
    Naipanoi, son of Nataana,
    Njeri, mother of Waragugu,
    Ireri, father of Mwara,
    Kanja, brother of Waceke,
    Wahu, mother of Kabir,
    Nyawira, sister of Kacey,

Kimba, son of the deep forest, twenty men hit us with fiery stones. The sound of thunder knocked us from our feet, and then brought silence. Can you hear me?

(Mlima listens to the voices with his entire body. He presses against his confinement of the container. The voices taunt him.)

MLIMA: I'm Mlima of the Great Plains. Eldest of my clan. I was tracked for many days, taken by a poison arrow. Why are there so many of you?! Mumbi? Koko? Do you hear me?

FAINT LAYERED VOICES:

Kade, Son of Gatimu,

Kabonessa, daughter of Kiserian,

Lakenua, mother of Namelok,

Naipanoi, son of Nataana, I crossed the desert to hide from a swarm of men. I didn't run fast enough to keep up with my mother. Mother, I'm sorry. I ran as fast as I could. I know you're sad.

Njeri, mother of Waragugu,

Ireri, father of Mwara,

Kanja, brother of Waceke,

Wahu, mother of Kabir,

Nyawira, sister of Kacey.

MLIMA: Too many voices, why don't I know you?

FAINT LAYERED VOICES:

Kade, son of Gatimu,

Kabonessa, daughter of Kiserian,

Lakenua, mother of Namelok,

Naipanoi, son of Nataana,

Njeri, mother of Waragugu, they took my child, and I couldn't leave her. I've seen what they do. I couldn't leave her. I could not leave her.

Ireri, father of Mwara,

Kanja, brother of Waceke,

Wahu, mother of Kabir,
Nyawira, sister of Kacey,
MLIMA: Mlima, father of Gitu.

(He fights to get out. It is a fight that he loses.)

XI

WHERE THERE IS BLOOD, THERE IS PLENTY OF FOOD

An austere customs office. A table, two chairs. Hai Phong, Vietnam.
Captain Ramaaker sits alone. Offstage voices argue, barely audible. He gets up, paces, sits, then gets up again. Finally, Hua Huynh, an officious customs officer, enters. He smokes a cigarette, and wears his hat cocked to the side.

HUA HUYNH: Sit. Sit.

(*A moment. Captain Ramaaker sits.*)

May I see your identification?

(*Captain Ramaaker gives him his ID.*)

CAPTAIN RAMAAKER: Can you tell me what this is all about? I'm only in Vietnam for another day. I haven't finished my logs // and I was hoping—

HUA HUYNH: Where are you coming from?

CAPTAIN RAMAAKER: Malaysia.

HUA HUYNH: Port of origin.

CAPTAIN RAMAAKER: Mombasa.

HUA HUYNH: Please show me your documents.

CAPTAIN RAMAAKER: Of course, as you can see all of the declarations and certificates for the containers are current and up to date.

(Hua Huynh carefully reviews the documents. Captain Ramaaker nervously watches.)

What's going on? Why am I being detained?

HUA HUYNH *(Reading)*: . . .

CAPTAIN RAMAAKER: Can you please tell me why I'm being—

HUA HUYNH: Everything is in order, but there is one container in question.

CAPTAIN RAMAAKER: Really? Which—

HUA HUYNH: Don Loc Enterprises.

CAPTAIN RAMAAKER: I . . . I don't recall all of the names of the companies.

HUA HUYNH: Did you inspect all of the containers?

CAPTAIN RAMAAKER: Yes. All of them.

CUSTOMS OFFICIAL: You did?

CAPTAIN RAMAAKER: . . . Yes. Is there a problem?

(Another customs agent enters, they whisper.)

HUA HUYNH: It appears you have no documentation for the . . . ivory.

CAPTAIN RAMAAKER: Ivory?! But, I'm not carrying ivory.

HUA HUYNH: The manifest lists the contents of this particular container as timber, but my inspectors examined it and found over a ton of ivory stowed beneath the wood.

CAPTAIN RAMAAKER *(Worried)*: . . .

HUA HUYNH: Again. Do you have the proper certificates for the ivory?

CAPTAIN RAMAAKER: . . . No. I don't. But I—

HUA HUYNH: This is all of your paperwork?

CAPTAIN RAMAAKER: Yes.

HUA HUYNH: You need further—

CAPTAIN RAMAAKER: Look. I wasn't aware that I was transporting ivory. This container must have been loaded without my knowledge. Sometimes it happens. I'm carrying a shit-load of cargo. And—

HUA HUYNH: Hmm. Because, you don't have the proper documentation, the ivory is considered contraband. And there are penalties.

CAPTAIN RAMAAKER: I have no idea how it got onto the ship. I just transport the cargo, I'm not responsible for what's inside the containers. Please. Please.

HUA HUYNH: You said you inspect each container?

CAPTAIN RAMAAKER: Yes, I do. I did. It's procedure.

HUA HUYNH: And?

CAPTAIN RAMAAKER: I don't know what to tell you.

HUA HUYNH: Can you confirm, that the consignee for this container is Don Loc Enterprises.

CAPTAIN RAMAAKER: I don't know. If that's what it says.

HUA HUYNH: Yes or no.

CAPTAIN RAMAAKER: . . . Yes, if that is what it states.

HUA HUYNH: Are you familiar with this particular company?

CAPTAIN RAMAAKER: I don't know. Perhaps. Can I make a telephone call? I'm sure I can clarify everything—

HUA HUYNH: Of course. Excuse me.

(Hua Huynh leaves.)

CAPTAIN RAMAAKER: Motherfucking hell. Son of a bitch.

(Captain Ramaaker resumes pacing. He then sits and buries his face in his hands.
Hua Huynh and the other customs agent reenter with Mlima. Captain Ramaaker immediately stands.)

HUA HUYNH: Sit. I'm afraid that you're going to have to remain here until the representative for Don Loc Enterprises arrives or—

CAPTAIN RAMAAKER: I have to coordinate // the loading of—

HUA HUYNH: I can't release you until I have further clarification. Unless there's something more that you wish to share.

CAPTAIN RAMAAKER: I can assure you that I had no prior knowledge of this transaction. You can look at my manifests. Is there someone else that I can speak to?

HUA HUYNH: Are you aware of the penalties for transporting contraband?

CAPTAIN RAMAAKER: . . . Yes.

(A moment. Hua Huynh stares at Captain Ramaaker, waiting for him to speak. Finally:)

HUA HUYNH: But, of course, there are fines that can be paid to avoid these problems.

CAPTAIN RAMAAKER: I'm sorry?

HUA HUYNH: Fines.

CAPTAIN RAMAAKER: . . . Oh.

HUA HUYNH: Do you understand?

CAPTAIN RAMAAKER: I do. Look, um, I didn't know—

HUA HUYNH: That doesn't matter.

CAPTAIN RAMAAKER: . . . I was not prepared.

HUA HUYNH: Perhaps, Mr. Loc will be better prepared.

CAPTAIN RAMAAKER: Perhaps.

HUA HUYNH: So what do you think we should do about this?

CAPTAIN RAMAAKER: You're asking me?

HUA HUYNH: I would like to know your opinion.

CAPTAIN RAMAAKER: The container is not mine, and therefore I take no responsibility for its contents. If things were to go missing, I couldn't vouch for them. Does that answer your question.

HUA HUYNH: That adds a great deal of clarity.

CAPTAIN RAMAAKER: To be clear, I'm not a friend of Don Loc.

HUA HUYNH: That is good news for both of us.

(Hua Huynh whispers something to the other customs agent, who immediately leaves.)

CAPTAIN RAMAAKER: Am I free to go?

HUA HUYNH: Your paperwork appears to be in order.

XII

THE MOUTH THAT EATS DOES NOT TALK

Carving shop. Hot. Vietnamese pop music provides ambient sound. Thuy Fan, a Vietnamese trader, wearing a T-shirt and shorts, fastidiously prepares tea. Hua Huynh sits at the table.
Mlima looms over their table.

THUY FAN: I was nervous when I got your call, usually I don't hear from you unless there's bad news.
HUA HUYNH: I thought you might be interested.
THUY FAN: I am. Very. Just a minute. *(Sips broth from a bowl)* I'm sorry. You caught me at the end of my meal. Tea?
HUA HUYNH: Thank you.
THUY FAN: Angie! Angie!

(Angie, the trader's wife, wearing headphones, aloof, enters. She serves them tea.)

HUA HUYNH: Hello, Angie.
ANGIE: Mr. Huynh.

(Angie retreats.)

THUY FAN: Well, I'm glad you called me first. This is a delicate situation. Will you take off your shirt?
HUA HUYNH: Why?
THUY FAN: For my comfort.

(Hua Huynh takes off his shirt. Thuy Fan pats down Hua Huynh.)

Forgive me, I never trust unearned good fortune. And if you're trying to fuck me, I will reach up your ass and rip out your heart.
HUA HUYNH: You have my word. I swear.

(A moment.)

THUY FAN: Good. The tusks are very special indeed. Generally, I would be angry! I don't like to step on the feet of others. BUT, I have a dealer in China who's been asking for quality. And because of the recent crackdowns it has become increasingly difficult to satisfy his taste.
HUA HUYNH: Then I'm happy that you are pleased.
THUY FAN: How does Mr. Loc feel about this?
HUA HUYNH: Mr. Loc is being cooperative. It was quite a large shipment for him. And he bypassed some important people, so he must be flexible.

(Thuy Fan laughs with pleasure.)

THUY FAN: Ah. That old fuck give you fight?
HUA HUYNH: He did, but in the end he had little choice. I leveled—

THUY FAN: The details aren't important. I know him well, and he's not going to be pleased. But I'm prepared.

(Angie returns and places a plate of food on the table.)

What is this?
ANGIE *(Curtly)*: Beef!

(She abruptly leaves. Mlima appears.)

THUY FAN: I've never seen a pair of tusks this wonderfully symmetrical. Outstanding. All of these years and it's nice that I can still be surprised. You forget what beauty can do for the spirit. Do you know of their origin?
HUA HUYNH: Mombasa. My guess, Kenya. Tanzania maybe.
THUY FAN: I should be angry at you for overstepping. But, today you've made me one of the happiest men in Vietnam. I have been wanting to stick it to Mr. Loc. Make that big cock limp!
HUA HUYNH: Boss. You said to keep my eyes open.
THUY FAN: You are a good boy. You did very well. Come, let me give you a kiss.

(Thuy Fan kisses Hua Huynh on both cheeks.)

The problem with Mr. Loc: He's too much of a businessman. He never stops to look and savor what he has. It's his flaw. Do you know why I do this?
HUA HUYNH: . . .
THUY FAN: Did you know that my father was Dung Nguyen, the great master carver?
HUA HUYNH: Yes, boss.
THUY FAN: He's the one that taught me to appreciate beauty. The emperor of Japan owns one of his carvings. It was a gift. It is true. I used to sit in the doorway of his workshop and watch him coax miracles from pieces of ivory. Do you

know why ivory is so special? Because it's soft, malleable. The carver can have a smooth conversation with the material, and rarely does it argue or fight back. Mr. Loc has a factory full of clumsy thumbs: workers, not artists. He makes carvings to satisfy greed, not the soul. And these special tusks are worthy of a master, and so you did right by bringing them to me.

(Thuy Fan strokes Mlima. He lifts him up. Lies him down.)

HUA HUYNH: I've seen many things in my job, but these took my breath away.
THUY FAN: Are there any certificates I should be aware of?
HUA HUYNH: Nothing.
THUY FAN: That's okay. I can manage the documents. Twenty thousand dong per kilogram.
HUA HUYNH: Twenty-two. It wasn't easy to move them out of customs without curious eyes.
THUY FAN: It must have been a mighty beast to surrender teeth this size.

(Hua Huynh leaves. Thuy Fan places a call on his cell phone.)

Master Yee? Yes. Thuy Fan. Yes. Thuy Fan. I have what you want!

XIII

RAIN BEATS A LEOPARD'S SKIN, BUT DOES NOT WASH OUT ITS SPOTS

Ivory factory.

Mlima stands in the middle of the stage. Master Yee walks around him, examines him, strokes him, taps him, and finally examines him with a magnifying glass. Thuy Fan watches.

MASTER YEE: I'm speechless. Honored that you've entrusted me with these magnificent tusks.

THUY FAN: I wanted you to see them in person, because I knew you wouldn't believe me.

MASTER YEE: Magnificent.

THUY FAN: What do you think?

MASTER YEE: My goodness—

THUY FAN: I feel the same way. Extraordinary.

MASTER YEE: This will be no easy task.

(Master Yee runs his hands up and down Mlima. It is sensual, intimate.)

I have too many thoughts. I haven't seen a pair of tusks like this in many many years. Not since I was a young man. Where . . . where did you find them?

THUY FAN: Rescued from the hands of a lesser craftsman who would have chipped away at its beauty. I felt there was only one man worthy of its grandeur.

MASTER YEE *(To Mlima)*: What should I do with you?

THUY FAN: You're the artist. You tell me.

MASTER YEE: I feel the tusks should be in conversation. Masculine and feminine. In a pair like this there is always one that is dominant, larger. Come look. A strong bull gave us these. Solid, gorgeous color. Smooth, and surprisingly unblemished. You see the rings, you can almost determine his age. About fifty years old. A savannah elephant, no doubt. Rare. Very rare. Most of the big tuskers are long gone. Extraordinary. I feel that something singular can be made from them.

THUY FAN: I am pleased to hear that.

MASTER YEE: Is there anything that I need to know before I begin?

THUY FAN: Why? Is there something wrong?

MASTER YEE: I'm cautious these days, the ban has made it hard to focus on my craft. Suddenly, I feel like a criminal for doing what I have always done.

THUY FAN: The officials don't know any better. I wouldn't worry.

MASTER YEE: I'm a Buddhist. I could not conscience killing for my craft. All of our pieces in the workshop, their provenance is clean, from older stockpiles. I need your assurance that this was procured in a legal and ethical manner.

THUY FAN: Yes, yes.

MASTER YEE: Since the ban, I will no longer touch anything that places the elephant in jeopardy.

THUY FAN: Of course. It was sitting in a warehouse, most of which was culled from before CITES was even signed. I rescued it for you, Master Yee.

MASTER YEE: That is all I need to know.

THUY FAN: I'm like you: As much as I love ivory, I abhor that notion of killing for it.

MASTER YEE: I am pleased to hear you say that. It feels better knowing that.

THUY FAN: Just make something beautiful, and I will find the perfect buyer.

(Thuy Fan leaves.

Master Yee goes through the motions of contemplating, then measuring Mlima.

We see Mlima being carved, the spirit being twisted and tortured.)

XIV

IT IS THE GOLD OF THE UNCOUTH AND THE WEALTHY

Beijing. Upscale ivory shop. Bright and opulent. Canned music.
    Alice Ying, nouveau riche, talks loudly into a bluetooth device for her cell phone, absently perusing the shop. Mr. Cheung, an obsequious salesman, trails closely behind her.
    Carved tusks on display. Fans. Landscapes, bracelets, buddhas, etc.

ALICE *(On cell phone)*: You keep telling me the same thing over and over again. Can you stop and listen to me for one minute? Yes, I'm going to buy something. That's right! How come you need to know? I'm at the Golden Pavilion right now. *(She point to a buddha)* How much?

MR. CHEUNG: Ten thousand yuan.

    (Alice gestures to her bluetooth device in her ear.)

I'm sorry.

ALICE *(On cell phone)*: I'm here. I'm here at the shop. Mr. Cheung say hello to Mr. Cui, so he doesn't think I'm with a lover.

MR. CHEUNG: Hello, Mr. Cui.

ALICE *(On cell phone)*: You want me to take a picture? You're crazy. So crazy.

(Alice takes a selfie with Mr. Cheung.)

(On cell phone) Hold on. Hold on. I am sending it now. I hope it shuts you up!! I'm looking at ivory sculptures. What do you want? For you! Everything's the same. Buddha laughing, Buddha singing, Buddha dancing, pretty landscape, pretty flowers, pretty birds, pretty dragon. I know. Yes, I will select something beautiful.

MR. CHEUNG: May I show you something?

(Alice gestures to her bluetooth device.)

ALICE *(On cell phone)*: I have to hang up. NOW! *(Hangs up)* These are pretty. How much?

MR. CHEUNG: Twenty thousand yuan.

FAINT LAYERED VOICES:

> Kade, son of Gatimu,
> Kabonessa, daughter of Kiserian,
> Lakenua, mother of Namelok,
> Naipanoi, son of Nataana,
> Njeri, mother of Waragugu,
> Ireri, father of Mwara,
> Kanja, brother of Waceke,
> Wahu, mother of Kabir,
> Nyawira, sister of Kacey.

ALICE: We purchased a new flat, penthouse and my husband wants something large in the foyer to welcome our guests.

MR. CHEUNG: Newlyweds?

ALICE: Hardly.

MR. CHEUNG: I believe I understand exactly what you're looking for. A statement piece. Something for an auspicious occasion.

ALICE: Exactly.

MR. CHEUNG: Please look around the shop, and then we can discuss.

ALICE: I want something new, no antiques. Brand new.

(We hear the faint whispers of the elephants.)

MR. CHEUNG: What you see is mostly older ivory from before the ban. *(Lowers his voice)* But, if it is new ivory, then it must be from a dead elephant, or the tusks fall out when they get old, but they always grow back like teeth. So needn't worry, our certificates are in order.

ALICE: You hear so many different things.

MR. CHEUNG: Most of which is wrong.

ALICE: I'll let you know.

MR. CHEUNG: Of course, of course. Will you allow me to show you something incredible. Carved by Master Yee, but it's from antique ivory. He's one of our last remaining masters.

(Mr. Cheung displays Mlima. Alice gasps.)

Only a handful of people have ever seen these. So, please don't let people know I showed them to you.

ALICE: Gorgeous.

MR. CHEUNG: Rare beauty. Unfortunately, I must say the price reflects their uniqueness.

ALICE: . . . How much?

MR. CHEUNG: They are both near perfection. It took over one year to carve the pair. I should be asking 7.4 million yuan. But, for you, I'm going to ask only 7 million yuan. It's because I know you will be back. Don't ask. I'm selling them as a pair to the right buyer. I hope it is you.

ALICE: . . .

MR. CHEUNG: No quality home is complete without a great piece of ivory.

ALICE: Just beautiful.

MR. CHEUNG: Move in closer, look at the craftsmanship.

ALICE: May I touch them?

MR. CHEUNG: Gently. They are fragile.

(Alice runs her hands over Mlima.)

ALICE: So smooth.

MR. CHEUNG: In the days of the emperor such fine carving was common, but today it has become harder to find work this delicate. I see the lady likes it very much.

ALICE: I do.

MR. CHEUNG: Then I would not be afraid of the cost. It is nothing compared to how you will feel when you look at them each morning. The question is what price are you willing to pay for beauty?

(Mr. Cheung leaves Alice to contemplate Mlima. It is an intimate moment.)

XV

A MAN'S GREED IS LIKE A SNAKE THAT WANTS TO SWALLOW AN ELEPHANT

Penthouse apartment. A party. Ambient chatter in the distance.
Two hip, young men admire the view of the city. Colorful lights fill the landscape.

HONG FENG: I've heard rumors.
LI JUN: Rumors? Hardly rumors.
HONG FENG: Then it's true?
LI JUN: You didn't hear it from me.
HONG FENG: I find it hard to believe? Five years ago he was
    begging for startup money, and now—
LI JUN: And can we talk about this view?

   (A moment. Agog.)

HONG FENG: I think this is about as high up as I can stand.

LI JUN: Yes, well, each year they build higher, as if they're trying to convene with the gods.

(A moment.)

HONG FENG: Hey man, have you seen the carvings?

LI JUN: Not yet. It's all anyone is talking about at the office. Nearly seven million yuan for the pair.

HONG FENG: Shit, no.

LI JUN: Yes.

HONG FENG: Really?

LI JUN: Yes.

HONG FENG: You know they couldn't be outdone by Jinjing Jin.

LI JUN: What do you think?

HONG FENG: I don't know, man, I'm a vegan. I gave up meat a couple of years ago and it doesn't sit right.

LI JUN: Hmm, yeah.

HONG FENG: And, the price is obscene.

LI JUN: But it's barely a ripple in his fortune. People like them—

(Alice, with cell phone, enters. Air kisses.)

ALICE: Can I ask you to come inside?

HONG FENG: Yes.

(Alice disappears inside.)

Shall we go in?

(Inside.)

ALICE: We are so pleased to welcome you to our new flat. This space would not feel like home until we invited our friends inside. So thank you. To mark this auspicious occasion we wanted to share something very special.

(Alice unveils Mlima. Gasps. Polite applause.
   Lights fade on all, but Mlima, on display.
   A long protracted moment. We contemplate Mlima.
   Sounds of the savannah intrude.)

XVI

THUNDER IS NOT YET RAIN

The savannah. Full moon.
    Mlima listens with his entire body.
    An elephant dance.

MLIMA *(Shouting)*: If you're listening, remember, I count forty-
    eight rains from memory, five summers of dried grass.
    Mumbi, if you can hear me, don't come to mourn me. Run!
    Run! RUN!

END OF PLAY

LYNN NOTTAGE is a playwright and screenwriter, and the first woman to be awarded two Pulitzer Prizes for Drama (for *Sweat* and *Ruined*). Her plays have been produced widely in the United States and throughout the world. Her works include *Clyde's*; the musical adaptation of *The Secret Life of Bees*, with lyrics by Susan Birkenhead and music by Duncan Sheik; the opera adaptation of her play *Intimate Apparel*, composed by Ricky Ian Gordon; *Mlima's Tale*; *Sweat* (Pulitzer Prize, Obie Award, Evening Standard Award, Susan Smith Blackburn Prize); *By the Way, Meet Vera Stark* (Lilly Award); *Ruined* (Pulitzer Prize, Obie Award, Lucille Lortel Award, New York Drama Critics' Circle Award, AUDELCO Award, Drama Desk Award, Outer Critics Circle Award); *Intimate Apparel* (American Theatre Critics Award, New York Drama Critics' Circle Award).

She developed and curated *This Is Reading*, a multimedia performance installation in Reading, Pennsylvania; and *The Watering Hole*, a multimedia performance installation at the Signature Theatre in New York City.

Her television credits include *She's Gotta Have It* (writer/producer, Netflix) and *Dickinson* (consulting producer, Apple TV).

Her honors include the PEN/Laura Pels Master American Dramatist Award, the Doris Duke Artist Award, a Literature Award from The American Academy of Arts and Letters, the MacArthur "Genius" Fellowship, a Guggenheim Grant, a Lucille Lortel Fellowship, the Steinberg "Mimi" Distinguished Playwright Award, the National Black Theatre Festival's August Wilson Playwriting Award, and a Lucille Lortel Sidewalk Star, among many others.

She is the co-founder of the production company Market Road Films, an associate professor in the Theatre Department at Columbia University School of the Arts, and a member of the American Academy of Arts and Letters, the American Academy of Arts and Sciences, and The Dramatists Guild.

Theatre Communications Group would like to offer our special thanks to The Repertory Theatre of St. Louis and its generous donors: Ann Scheuer, Ann Cady Scott, Pat and Ken Schutte, Gwen and Paul Middeke, Lori Moore-McMullen and Kevin McMullen (in memoriam), Wendi Alper-Pressman and Norman Pressman, Susan and Peter Tuteur, and Judi Scissors and Sam Broh, for their support of the publication of Mlima's Tale *by Lynn Nottage.*

The Repertory Theatre of St. Louis is dedicated to excellence in producing an eclectic range of live theatre.

tcg